Disruptive Change

Disruptive Change

HOW NEW POWER IS TRANSFORMING A BACKWARD CIVILIZATION

—⁂—

The Futurist Series

J. M. Docks

Cover Design by Katie Geary (KatieGeary.com)

ISBN: 1532705778
ISBN 13: 9781532705779

To my God, who makes all things possible, and to the future generations.
To my godmother, the late Gwendolyn K. Banks, whom I love and miss.

Table of Contents

Introduction

—⁂—

PRESENT CIRCUMSTANCES LEAD US TO believe the inevitable imminence of drastic changes in the way the world operates. This means, among other things, the growing influence of new models in society—models that will redefine for generations, and perhaps for a few centuries, the very meaning and purpose of life itself. These new models—and their heirs, the youth—struggle at present to liberate themselves from the confinements of an old order, long believed to be on its last leg, which constructed for countless souls a reality revolving around a simple, crude model. This is to say, the past few hundred years have been defined by a monotonous routine of evolution; the meaning of life encompassed in the axiom of birth, growth, maturation, decline, and death—a straight shot in a vicious cycle. Along this path, it has been the general expectation that humankind become educated for the purposes of labor in order to reproduce a family and pass on the very same values and processes before the certainty of retirement—if fortunate—and ultimately death.

Thought for its time to be superior, innovative, and progressive, this era has proven itself creatively destructive and crude—advanced on a technological level, yet primitive in its humanity. It has subsequently limited its potential for exploration and innovation, thus curtailing its greatness, as antiquity will surely show. We have long lived in a world that values security from scarcity over everything else—fear being the underlying emotion of our existence. This fear has been compressed within the boundaries of currency and power—that is to say, we have sought to protect ourselves from our insecurities through riches and control. Considered to be a by-product of "natural" laws (Darwin's theory of evolution by natural selection: those individuals with heritable traits better suited to the environment will survive; that is, *survival of the fittest* as Herbert Spencer terms it), we have constructed a world that combined positive and negative elements—creativity and antisocial behavior, for example—in order to innovate and expected these elements to produce optimal solutions. And while, indeed, the model of *old power* worked in many respects during its time—either because it was superior, or by other means—its elemental framework is now mired in disintegrative obsolescence on a material and technological level, but especially on a psychological and emotional one.

As disintegration continually leads to crises globally, a new model of social organization is restructuring societies and changing the way we think about innovation, governance, and particularly people and purpose—our *raison d'être*. With an emphasis on collaboration, diversity, decentralization, and interconnectedness, *new power* presents fresh opportunities for the globe to reinvent its structures at every level. This opportunity presents itself in the form of disruption—that is, disruptive change.

The first sign of disruption exists within the magnifying shifts in the consciousness of individuals; this psychological swing in momentum is particularly noticeable in the youth of the modern world. It was B. F. Skinner who observed that "society attacks early, when the individual is helpless."[1] That, via the process of socialization, the old-power model directed by the paternalism of authority (i.e., the state, corporations, boards of education, etc.) made a straight-cut ditch out of free, meandering brooks. We were told that the world worked only one or two ways, and the capacity for imagination and creativity was thus limited within the model as specified. Mistaking liberty for freedom, generations embarked upon life's pursuit under the assumption that the fruit of the old order was both innovative and unprecedented. We revered our gas-guzzling automobiles; our skyscrapers made of glass; our cameras, televisions, and computers; our lattes; our designer apparel; our bank accounts; our vacation spots; our wry white-collar, blue-collar humor; and money itself over the imperative questions of impact: What do I desire? What is my place in the universe? What if money is no object? This has been, as a synopsis, the overarching pattern of the past era. Nevertheless, the vibrational current that is new power has instilled within the coming generations a growing desire for something more than this superficiality.

As a scientist and India's eleventh president, A. P. J. Abdul Kalam once eloquently enunciated the very essence of the new-power consciousness:

> A characteristic feature of the authoritarianism in our society is its insidious ability to addict people to the endless pursuit of external rewards, wealth, prestige, position, promotion, approval of one's lifestyle by others, ceremonial honors, and status symbols of all kinds. To successfully pursue these goals, they have to learn elaborate rules of etiquette and familiarize themselves with customs, traditions, protocols and so on. The youth of today must unlearn this self-defeating way of life. The culture of working only for material possessions and rewards must be discarded. Are you aware of your inner signals? Do you trust them? Have you taken control over your life into your own hands? Take this from me, the more decisions you can make avoiding external pressures, which will constantly try to manipulate you, the better your life will be, the better your society will become. Life is a difficult game. You can only win by retaining your right to be a person. And to retain this right, you will have to be willing to take the social or external risks involved in ignoring pressures to do things the way others say they should be done.[2]

Simply put, we are here to change the world, not to follow rules, earn money, and die—a revolution in interpersonal sentiment that will necessarily reconfigure the forms and structures of the old orders by its very nature alone. Old power was mistaken, which even Darwin himself avowed: "It is not the strongest of the species that survives, nor the most intelligent that survives. It is the one that is most adaptable to change."[3] Therefore, what this new consciousness is producing is a greater yearning for freedom (not to be confused with liberty)—freedom from all limitations. This is a feat that can at present only be accomplished with new models and frameworks for the execution of new goals and desires—a new life's purpose.

It was commonly predicted that the youth of the past decades would possess no future because of unfavorable political and economic circumstances. Safe to say, this is proving to be outstandingly false, as it originally was. It turns out that it's actually a wonderful time to be alive. This comes in correlation with the accelerating disintegration of institutions and thinking, which have long been antiquated and are, at present, manifesting themselves as such.

This acceleration of change—or in some circumstances, shock—has emerged in every core aspect of modern civilization from energy, technology, and government to family life and moral attitudes. The pace at which this is occurring has affected the minds of different people in different ways. For some, it has awakened a robust nostalgia, a reactionary conservatism longing for the "good ol' days." This yearning separates sympathizers merely by how far into the past they would wish to push us—some want the 1980s and the 1990s back, while others desire the 1950s; still others long for delusions of grandeur and for agrarian or medieval utopias, and so forth. On the other hand, there are those who see the future through the lenses of unrealistic expectations as a technological utopia run by "benevolent" global institutions—an extension of the failed bureaucratic thinking of times past. Nevertheless, present trends are gradually upending the expectations of both camps into the seas of disruption. The next several decades present us with not only unprecedented challenges but also unparalleled opportunities. This short work is therefore the expressive declaration by the change-making youth of this generation, enunciating the necessary transformations of what is for us a backward and outdated civilization being transfigured through disruptive change.

Change is not, as has been advertised to us, light, airy, and easy. To the contrary, "All great changes are preceded by chaos."[4] If progress is meaningful—that is, revolutionary in impact as opposed to reformatory—it will of necessity dispel the comfortable stagnancy that is the status quo. For if people do not refashion themselves, time itself has a way of bringing about a change; either way, disruption becomes unavoidable as changing circumstances inexorably clash with the passé. Such a time is this.

What we are conveying in this text is a conversion occurring in the cognitive landscape—that is, the way people think. As each year goes by, these changes are becoming increasingly noticeable and disruptive to existing conditions. This disruption has not only manifested itself in the form of crises within representative and governance institutions—for example, the "Government Shutdown" in October of 2013, or the subtle political implications of the Flint Water Crisis (government failure at every level)—but has also competed for supremacy in production and creativity—for example, the future prospects of robotics and automating the workforce or the endless possibilities of breakthroughs like virtual reality. As breakthroughs in energy (e.g., Tesla's successful and legitimate commercialization of superior electric automotive technology), finance and currency (e.g., Kickstarter offers perhaps the first glance into the future of finance and funding without banks), transportation (e.g., Uber, the world's premier private transportation company owns no cars), and information (e.g., Wikipedia) continue, the old institutions have and will attempt to absorb, buy out, or destroy these new forms in an effort to survive. Yet, as the innovations continue, these institutions will be outrun by both the limitlessness of creators and the shifting demands of global populations. Such institutions will inevitably be forced to face the narrow prospects of capitulation or permanent obsolescence. This is because the disruptive change that is occurring is converging globally, creating a new synthesis that will replace the dominant values and mores of the past three-hundred-plus years.

Our aim here is to provide a simple framework explaining the necessity of these adaptations and where they just might be headed. Ours is therefore a position of consciousness as well as a material one.

As change agents, we feel it less appropriate to bore readers with the obvious alterations that have accompanied the technological and productive transitions over recent times. This is obvious. It is clear that the world is changing at a rapid pace; it seems as if nothing lasts anymore. MySpace made its introduction in August 2003, generating significant buzz at its peak but was quickly eclipsed by Facebook only a few years later. Now, MySpace is ancient history in twenty-first-century terms. In many senses, this is not only astounding from a mental standpoint, in that such a rapid change in the way people connect and share information could shift so much over such a short time, but it also demystifies the lazy presumption that the way the world looks and works today is the way it will look and work forever. Thus, the lesson should be clear: everything is transient; the only constant is change.

The former is but a small example of the larger picture; inevitably, what we are witnessing is the cumulative transformation of contemporary society. A world rooted in the proclivities of industrialism, which in conjunction with the productive and energy dependencies of the industrial era, standardized, synchronized, specialized, centralized, concentrated, maximized, and commercialized every aspect of life. The intricate and intersecting aspects of this order created what we could term a "value-maximization society"—a society comprehensively saturated by the influence, and ultimately accumulation, of money in all aspects of life including politically (e.g., the campaign for public office) and socially—which is reinforced by economic imperatives like rent, taxation, consumptive taxes, the cost of education and a myriad of costs, fee's, penalties and debt obligations. It is, in short, an old power set of ideological assumptions of the industrial era, which, like all life-forms, has run its course.

As with any life-form whose existence is threatened by metamorphosis, the ultimate decision comes down to whether old institutions will join the new wave of social development or wither away. Regardless of the choice made, this disruptive change will transform all aspects of ordinary life, including the way we work, play, communicate, govern, travel, live, and love. It is, in essence, a (televised) revolution. However, what has made the so-called revolutions of aforetime largely ineffective (or in some cases, destructive) has been their misunderstanding of the core principle of change; that is to say, change is often the result of a series of small but consistent adjustments, as opposed to one violent and sudden upheaval. Change is in the process of stages, however short or long. That being said, we will innovate, not force, our way into the next epoch.

However, it is important to make a relevant clarification. In the Western world, we are socialized to conceive of time as being linear— that is, having a beginning and end, an A to B, a start to an end. What has accompanied this, in turn, is the presumption of progress; in other words, as time moves forward, humanity is expected to be socially, politically, economically, and technologically superior to the preceding generations. The past is history, the present is past, and the future is now and almost always better. This has been accompanied by expectations that not only has our modern technosocial development superseded the past (de facto) but that the continuance of these developments, of themselves, will finally enable us to resolve problems that never could have been fixed before. We are, so the narrative goes, gradually inching toward perfection—that is, the end of war, disease, hunger, and poverty (if we're perfect). Nevertheless, this defeats the purpose. If at this point only along the process of human evolution we are just now capable of resolving the dilemmas of humanity with technology and complex concepts, just how primitive is humanity yet still in its historical development? This one-size-fits-all means of problem solving—especially via the "saviors" of technology and economic growth—doesn't exhibit superior development; instead, it is the mark of a lack of sophistication and creative capacity, one that is as emotional as it is logical.

Disruptive change is exhilarating, not because it will solve all problems but because it gives us the opportunity to right some of our most obvious historical wrongs and avoid ghastly tragedies in the future. This is a phenomenon we see occurring through the lens of emerging new-power dynamics in contradistinction to old-power institutions and methods. Of course this process will not be without conflict and crisis. Progressivism presumes that the past is by nature backward and primitive and that the future is, by consequence, advanced and positive. It presumes that technology is the ultimate force of history, that time is linear, and that by progression humanity can resolve its ills in total through its material development in deference to its psychological or social development. These suppositions are neither guaranteed nor logically sound.

We argue that although progress, or more appropriately, the future (a continuum in the cycle of time), presents great possibilities, there is no guarantee that tomorrow will be better than today or yesterday a priori. Indeed, the emergence of new-power trends and the disruption of old-power dynamics present for us the hopeful prospects of a world absent of the drudgeries and tyrannies of the modern world. Nevertheless, if antiquity is a lesson at all, we know too well that new ideas and new ways of life bring with them novel drudgeries and tyrannies in equal proportion to new liberations and peace. Thus, we want to present a general framework documenting how new-power trends are transforming the way we live, as well as present concepts as to what measures we can take to ensure that the development of this new wave is generally beneficial and not counterintuitive.

A New Psychosphere

—ɯ—

MANY OF THE SO-CALLED CRISES the modern world is experiencing come from an awareness of significant, if not unprecedented transformations in the way of living across borders, but a general ignorance and anxiety as to where these changes will lead specifically. Everything seems to be moving so fast—job layoffs, political violence, diplomatic conflict, technological disruption, and so on—but it's difficult to define what all of this means. And for peace of mind, unfounded speculation will not do. This is neither unreasonable nor unexpected. Any substantial change, before it materializes, begins in the heart and mind first—a sort of internal disruption. As the new wave continues to materialize, the world will perpetually experience surmounting crises of inter- and intrapersonal behavior and communications; that is to say, change is changing the way we think and interact.

At present, the reactionary trend toward disruptive change, especially concerning the youth, has been one of crippling despair; when asked if their generation would have a better life than their parents, a recent survey found that youth in developing countries (Brazil, Russia, India, China, etc.) were far more optimistic about the future than their counterparts in developed countries.[5] A young Chinese woman confidently asserted, "I really do believe that things are getting better, both for my age group and for society as a whole."[6] But not so in other geographies. In other circumstances, disruption has engendered a subtle and persistent inner tension. While the twenty-first century will witness an increasing shift of power to the East—the future of geopolitics is sure to be multipolar—we believe, rather, that the deepest roots of our general unease can be traced to fundamental metamorphoses in the models underpinning societies' ways of life (psychologically and materially).

The old-power era erected itself upon at least two principles (not at all comprehensive): (1) reliance upon and obedience to authority and (2) value maximization (the accumulation of money as the primary motivation of all institutions and social relations—"everything costs")—a reinforcement of the longevity of the former. In each case, the average individual was subjected by his or her environment to the paternalism of the state and large financial and/or commercial institutions. It was generally regarded that the administration, the committee, the bureau, the board, the council, the shareholders, the board of directors, or the managers—whatever one's ideological vice—knew best. It was the job of individuals to take orders and produce monetary returns (i.e., value maximization) for their respective institutions, using their ingenuity and creative capacities in the context of these existing forms and under the presiding rules of engagement. And it is via old power that societies were built after the character of industrialism—dependent upon authority and willing to follow and obey.

Under these conditions, things like individuality, diversity, or a radical cultural equality were ostracized characteristics in favor of a mass identity—characteristics now odiously rejected with ignominy. It is here that old power garnished its familiar characteristics, as elaborated by Jeremy Heimans and Henry Timms: power held by a few, leader-driven, closed, and heavily reliant on dominance—"Old power downloads and commands."[7] This is, more or less, the narrative that has interpreted the universe to us for at least the past half millennia. But immediately, we find ourselves in a dilemma. The by-product of disruptive change in the age of information—with its networks (for example, the Internet or the advent of social media platforms) and instant communication or feedback—is a continual grasping, generally, for independence upon the part of the individual over the influences in their lives; a complete reversal of a previous wave given to uniformity across all categories (mass culture, consumption and thinking). However, as new-power dynamics continue to manifest within older structures (think Uber's flexibility versus the rigid banality of the taxi industry), and as these models, depending on the level of peer coordination and mass participation, make people feel more powerful and independent, we find that people tend to want more not less of the same. "New power uploads and shares,"[8] and surprisingly (well, not really), people actually enjoy having autonomous control and participatory influence over their lives. This creates a psychological and material frustration because standing in the way of these desires is a more traditional means of doing things. It is the old model. Institutions built for a uniform and obedient audience are now entertaining a constituency, which is the exact opposite; increasingly variable and self-determining. This has reactively led to an internal repression—a desiring for something more (e.g., more control, more autonomy, more independence) blocked indefinitely by circumstances and customs, in other words, a dream deferred. Subsequently, societies have gradually arrived at psychological disruption: a state of consciousness torn between two worlds—stuck in one, desiring to be in another.

Because "the balance of power is shifting,"[9] new power, with its radical transparency, demand for informal governance, and commitment to collaboration for its own sake, is shaping a new psychosphere (the way nations and peoples think about the world) foreshadowed best by millennials and their historically unique position. Having surpassed baby boomers as one of the largest populations in history, millennials are special because of their cultural inheritance (they are the most racially diverse generation in US history for example[10])—they're the first digital natives and are the most socially connected group globally. Nevertheless, because of the tumultuous political and economic circumstances that they've inherited, millennials have less money to spend than previous generations (e.g., student debt), and have put off certain milestones in their lives like home ownership and marriage (according to a 2013 Pew research study, 36 percent of young people eighteen to thirty still live with parents[11]). Circumstances have subsequently led them to resort to innovative thrift as a means of survival—for example, a Goldman Sachs poll in 2013 found that 30 percent of millennials polled have no intention of purchasing their own vehicle in the near future, and only 25 percent agreed that car ownership was important but not a big priority.[12] The evidence of an emerging psychosphere rests in millennials' strategic reactions toward circumstantial obstacles such as these, which have resulted in nothing less than a disruptive change (psychological disruption = material fruit). As a response to the dilemma of transportation, what has emerged is the concept that access is more important than ownership; that ride-sharing (services like Uber, Zip Car & Relay Rides) can supplant or even surpass the nuances of owning a vehicle, all things being equal. While but one small example, the foreseeable end of these developments is nothing less than a domino effect of possibilities. If it is true, as author and economist Jeremy Rifkin said, that "Twenty-five years from now, car sharing will be the norm, and car ownership an anomaly,"[13] what effect would such attitudes as "access > ownership" have on the future of urban planning in designing cities, or on civil engineering and architecture? How does this subtle power shift in world view spread to other sectors such as the automotive industry, finance, or home ownership (real estate)? And how does it fuse with technology? Given the gradual but consistent shifts in critical thinking (how we approach twenty-first century problems with twenty-first- and (even) twenty-second-century answers), the possibilities are endless.

Although the use of "examples" is traditionally a persuasive tool, it is imperative to emphasize that the significant reforms in industries such as transportation, though of "minute" consequence now, are, in the grand scheme of it all, demonstrations of the small, lustrous and steady gesticulations that characterize historical periods of real transformative change. In repetition, evolution is not defined by sudden upheaval, but is the culmination of small and consistent transformations over time. In our case, these gestures are evidences not merely of technological advancement or innovative thrift, but the results of the changing paradigm that will become the twenty-first century.

It isn't merely our reaction to circumstances like car ownership that's changing, but the thinking underpinning our reactions in the first place. Case in point, the world views that characterized the previous wave was particularly insistent on doctrines such as the Protestant ethic—deferral of gratification, emphasis on thrift, a lifetime of physically arduous hard work—and other cultural traditions in order to channel mass energy into industrial and postindustrial economic growth. Most of these ideological influences are still observable today, as for example, the roots of the startup entrepreneur niche—its "sleep is for the weak" and eighty- to one-hundred-hour-workweek mantras—have their ultimate origins in Calvinistic theology and Max Weber's Spirit of Capitalism or beyond. Nevertheless, what the Protestant ethic and maturation of scientific and industrial development was to the time before it, disruptive change is poised to do as of now.

While as of yet we lack a specific name for this emerging psychological phenomenon, it is clear we are swiftly moving away from the Orwellian uniformity the past era presented us. The standardization and synchronization of life—at the pace and time at which the industrial world demanded—is no longer the standard and we are instead transforming into its opposite. We are moving, in a word, to a greater *diversification* of society. A product of the next psychosphere, diversification is an increasing proliferation of differences among the populations of nations and cultures; where diversity is a distinguishing feature of nations both figuratively and literally. Not only is this distinguishable by trends in immigration (by 2055 the United States will be without a single racial/ethnic majority[14]), or politics (the 2016 electorate is, to-date, the most diverse in US history with 50 percent of millennials identifying as "independent" of either mainstream political party[15]), but also in production—as the demand for standardized goods from a mass market is being replaced by unique goods for more specific niches. Companies are increasingly relying upon data and the metrics they provide to track consumer-specific spending habits—in the grocery store (e.g., the bar-code) or online—in order to advertise according to customers unique proclivities; the pop-up Google ads on your Internet browser, which reflect search history and consumer preferences is a good example. These material progressions, notwithstanding, occur in sync with the intangible, psychological transformations that will become the future of societies. Diversification has subsequently had the inadvertent consequence of magnifying the role and value of the individual psychologically and culturally. The culmination of a great domino effect; individuals increasingly concern themselves with self-discovery, the meaning of life, adventure, and balance—slowly redefining conceptions of "success"—while deemphasizing the monotonous value-systems characterizing old power. This also means an increasing influence in do-it-yourself culture and "meaning over money" as a new philosophy of life—that is to say, individuals and young people in particular, will actively seek out economically productive lives that fulfill them emotionally and financially at once, with more emphasis upon the former. In other words, the advent of diversification represents an end to mass industrial civilization designed to create uniformity in every sector of society. In the future, differences won't only be accepted, they'll flourish. Among other elements, this is a sociopolitical and economic imperative to globalization in the new millennium.

Nevertheless, as we continue to delve into the depths of the new psychosphere, we will continually experience a series of "crises" in the midst of transition. Though the future product of disruptive change will produce societies that embrace diversity, or others that radically redefine the importance and significance of individualism, for now the reality of this future in the present proves difficult. While the psychosphere that is new power will emphasize tolerance, the payoff for a representative victory—especially as the "representation market" saturates—is often a sociocultural isolation. This is because as family structures continually change for example, (nuclear families, traditionally defined, will become a thing of the past) it necessitates, also, a change in values and morals. And while the reduction of religious affiliation for millennials (research shows they're far less religious than older generations[16]), or the political victory of marriage equality foreshadows things to come, values as a rule are slower to change than material reality. Thus, the shifting demographics and ethics of the next wave suffer from a violent intolerance or rejection in the present. Combine this with the contradiction of social technology (text messaging, IM, Chat, online social communities, etc.) and its impending loneliness epidemic—research suggests loneliness may become the next public health issue, alongside obesity and substance abuse[17]—and one will see that disruptive change has yet to mature in its totality.

This obstacle of consciousness however is only a temporary phenomenon concomitant with the novelty of old powers' disintegration; our minds have not fully evolved to the conditions of the next wave:

> One clue to the plague of loneliness lies in our rising level of social diversity. By de-massifying society, by accentuating differences rather than similarities, we help people individualize themselves. We make it possible for each of us more nearly to fulfill his or her potential. But we also make human contact more difficult. For the more individualized we are, the more difficult it becomes to find a mate or a lover who has precisely matching interests, values, schedules, or tastes. Friends are also harder to come by. We become choosier in our social ties. But so do others. The result is a great many ill-matched relationships. Or no relationships at all.
>
> The breakup of mass society, therefore, while holding out the promise of much greater individual self-fulfillment, is at least for the present spreading the pain of isolation.[18]

Nevertheless, while the individual as an entity is in the midst of re-invention our disruption in consciousness spills over into the political and socioeconomic workings of the modern world as well. There is, ultimately, a struggle for power that is increasingly manifesting; the result of psychological disruptive changes. Recent disruptions (of sociopolitical thought) such as the Occupy Movement, WikiLeaks, Snowden and the National Security Agency files, or police brutality and the Black Lives Matter response are visible indications that as disintegrative crises progress, old power, much like the hegemons before its time, will seek to protect its interests through reactionary measures by attempting to tighten its grip on elements it deems unruly. While the reactionary phenomenon is likely to increase in scale and violence as disintegration and the interests of the next wave becomes more explicit, it will, at the same time, accelerate the demand and actuation of the new psychosphere materially and emotionally.

Old-power models often required little more than passive consumption. Power was enabled by what people or organizations own, know, and control that nobody else does. This is why the principle of scarcity has been so relatively vital to the old-power, value-maximization societies—secret advantages being the key to wealth and power. However, with new powers religious devotion to transparency, and the desire to tap into people's potential on a more self-determining level, these old advantages will no longer assuage a vibrant global citizenry. "Power is not just flowing differently; people are feeling and thinking differently about it."[19] This means societies are reacting differently to their institutions as well as themselves; and the entrenched establishments of old power must necessarily capitulate concessions to new institutions whose ideological, political, sexual, educational, theological, ethnic and cultural diversity materializes in fact as equally as it does in name. No less will do for the security and order of the twenty-first century.

Thus, the greatest struggle upon which new power and disruption will embark, is the evolution of values (legal and moral) upon which the next psychosphere will be defined. Heimans and Timms write critically:

The battle ahead, whether you favor old or new power values, will be about who can control and shape society's essential systems and structures. Will new power forces prove capable of fundamentally reforming existing structures? Will they have the ingenuity to bypass them altogether and create new ones? Or will they ultimately succeed in doing neither, allowing traditional models of governance, law, and capital markets to basically hold firm?[20]

Subsequently, as new power remains in search of its means to power—that is, moving from rhetoric to governance—our familiarity and comfort with orthodox representative and commercial institutions will inevitably undergo serious reconfigurations in engineering and aesthetics. "To truly transform government, new power will need to do more than change the short-term political dynamics—it must change the rules of the game."[21] Incidents such as the polarizing Brexit decision—a 51.9 percent to 48.1 percent vote by Britain's electorate to leave the EU—and its subsequent consequences (on civil politics, international trade and national culture) are illustrations of the imminent atmosphere of civil affairs and gauges of new powers *real* potential. As changes in the psychosphere allude—autonomous populaces no longer exclusively leaning upon old-power figureheads (politicians, multinationals, and mass media) for direction—the global citizenry is by no means sanguine. In the coming years, it should surprise no one that the general public will become increasingly opinionated concerning affairs once considered to be official state or commercial business, and they will look for a means to see that those opinions materialize; as the former example doth show. The state no longer enjoys a comfortable monopoly; it can no longer think for the people but must think with them. This subsequently marks a serious shift in the dynamics of power that are sure to have long-reaching consequences across all sectors of contemporary nationhood.

The Next Economic Synthesis

—ɯɯ—

IN ORDER FOR THE NEW millennium to thrive and reach its full potential, it will have to discard the nineteenth- and twentieth-century political and economic frameworks upon which old power relies. This is regardless of new power's uncertain influence; the structural makeup of the globe has shifted in such a way that current and future dilemmas cannot be addressed with the same methods. Taxing to supplant budget deficits, direct manipulation of the money supply through interest rates or other industrial era policies won't due. Simply put: "We cannot solve our problems with the same level of thinking that created them."[22] This is equally true for how we trade goods and services as it is for anything else. Thus, the greatest disruption of all will take place in how we view money, capital and exchange; and we've already seen early premonitions. Although we've only scratched the surface with psychological and material disruptions like the sharing economy—in which access > ownership (that has brought us notable companies as Airbnb and Uber)—disruptive change gradually produces new developments with the potential to take us deeper. Digital currencies, like Bitcoin, are not merely convenient alternatives to the traditional use of fiat or hard coinage, but are the perfect epitome of economy in the age of information; both as it is and as it has yet to be. What is poised to be the future of payments, the value of one digital Bitcoin alone had increased to as much as \$1,216 in 2013 only five years' time from the inception of cryptocurrencies.[23] Though temporarily derailed the following year by the ghastly Mt. Gox bankruptcy (a \$460 million catastrophe),[24] to prematurely prophesy the death of digital currencies revolution is both hyperbolic and shortsighted. The seed of an idea has been planted; what if a decentralized system of currency that facilitates exchange cheaper and easier, can substitute and exceed the old central banking monopolies that expand or shrink the money supply at will, which enormously influence economic activity? With the potential of inheriting a new air of respectability by a new wave of entrepreneurs, cashless cash and its economic consequences not only democratizes finance—contracting government control over money— but embodies the shifting ideals of the new psychosphere—its demand for greater autonomy—and the extensive powers of the Internet, which has somewhat democratized access to capital. Bitcoin's several copycats and the inauguration of information as the new driver of commerce not only show that digital money will persist but also intuitively suggest imminent disruptive changes over the coming years.

This is exceptionally significant because it represents a potential break from the value-maximization models that define old-power economies and their ethics. As disruption progressively scrambles what is the market triumph fairy tale, the current of change will enable the exposure of such ideas that transcend the predominate economic thinking of our time—to finally think differently about markets, capital, currency, and our relationship to exchange beyond the capitalism vs. socialism argument (as both are outdated, products of the last wave). Data as presented in works like Thomas Piketty's *Capital in the 21st Century* reveal the obvious fallacies of political economy as formerly practiced. The problems of old powers disintegrating economic infrastructure aren't just obvious, they're also burdening; with inequality at the forefront. Piketty's thesis that when the rate of return on capital is greater than the rate of economic growth the result is a concentration of wealth inevitably leading to unequal

distributions of wealth and socioeconomic instability, thoroughly de-
scribes the consequences of the old power crisis. Economic growth in
the coming decades presents its own dilemma as "developing countries will continue to grow more rapidly than the rich countries,"
remarked Ford Foundation and Harvard professor, Dani Rodrik, and
yet, "the kind of growth rate that developing countries experienced
until very recently is extremely, extremely rare...if you look at the
period before 1950, virtually no country in the world experienced
growth rates that were 4–4.5 percentage points on a per capita basis."[25] Whereas rapid industrialization could account for much of the
economic prosperity that characterized the last wave, the industrial
paradigm is history along with the economic conditions that characterized it; GDP growth rates for most developed countries are fore-
casted between 2–4 percent or less in the next five years, themes that
will become regrettably familiar.[26] That said, unlike Piketty's thesis
new power must get at the root of our problems (excessive inequality is a symptom not a cause) instead of skimming the surface—an
opportunity disruption will enable. Disruptive change thus presents
us the chance to reevaluate our economic infrastructure—its ethics of value-maximization (whose need for infinite growth will only
worsen inequality over the coming years)—and amend our relation
to capital and currency both economically and socially. That is to say,
if we redefine the underlying motivations of commerce (emphasizing
innovation, scientific inquiry and creativity over the accumulation
of value for its own sake) we could broaden the access to capital and
esoteric knowledge responsible for gross socioeconomic inequity in
the first place; especially in the information age. Or that the communication prowess of the Internet could be used to engender a spirit of
free enterprise, that microfunding platforms like Kickstarter could
be augmented and systematically incorporated into our economies
to accentuate and prosper the virtual entrepreneurship that will
characterize the millennium; including new tax incentives and legal
loopholes.

Thus, while disintegration continues, new solutions will have to be presented to avoid global catastrophes of political economy, because the future of work is not in corporate employment but in entrepreneurship[27] and a healthy economic atmosphere—philosophically, psychologically, and materially—can only lead to healthy societies, at home and abroad. As "millennials are realizing that starting a company, even if it crashes and burns, teaches them more in two years than sitting in a cubicle for 20 years,"[28] says Fred Tuffile Bentley University's Entrepreneurial Studies program director, a means must be created for generations who are overwhelmingly seeing starting their own business as the key to economic success. If virtual entrepreneurship (business done via the Internet) is the lifeline of the next generation of enterprisers, the old power vanguard must be prepared to make room. Thus, with components such as currency being the buttress of the global economy, it should come as no surprise that the elimination of traditional banking could and should be a tangible goal of twenty-first-century disruption for something that better suits the needs of virtual entrepreneurs and/or global citizens generally. This includes the abrupt irrelevance of our old ideological debates:

> The Second Wave gave rise to the first truly national markets and the very concept of a national economy. Along with these came the development of national tools for economic management—central planning in the socialist nations, central banks and national monetary and fiscal policies in the capitalist sector. Today both these sets of tools are failing—to the mystification of the Second Wave economists and politicians who try to manage the system.[29]

The truth is that just like the emerging psychosphere, the economies of the twenty-first century are being subjected to diversification in which only decentralized economic management will harmonize in the next synthesis though now it seems global and uniform, and the fact is not yet appreciated. Alvin Toffler referred to these as the breaking down of national economies into regional and sectorial parts in which subnational economies develop distinctive needs and problems of their own.[30] The needs and demands of Silicon Valley are uniquely divergent from that of a financial center like Wall Street or Tokyo (with its world-class factories, development labs and state-of-the-art research) as compared to London. Thus, as opposed to homogenizing as during the industrial era, the next wave of commerce moves in the opposite direction; "there is no one US economy," asserts Michael Porter of the Clinton Global Initiative, "but a collection of local economies," and so it is across the globe.[31]

> Failure to recognize this accounts in good measure for the bankruptcy of government efforts to stabilize the economy. Every attempt to offset inflation or unemployment through nationwide tax rebates or hikes, or monetary or credit manipulation, or through other uniform, undifferentiated policies, merely aggravates the disease.[32]

Instead, the next synthesis is creating a new set of rules with the opportunity to redefine what we're producing for. It provides us an occasion to ask critical questions such as the following: Why do we work? Is the corporate cubicle culture the greatest means to maximize people's talents? Is the end of all trade money or something beyond monetary value? Why do we pay rent? Should college education cost? Does the purchase of a home or car require the accumulation of large debts? It is a vindicating moment, as we believe, to replace the oppugnant features of value-maximization economies (lopsided taxation, deficit spending, inflationary fiat currency, sticky wages, gross inequality, scarcity of capital, the "rat race"), which is both counterintuitive to the proliferation of exchange in relations of commerce generally and pathologically ruinous to the cultural and social well-being of global populations. From a futuristic perspective we should see the pathology of the value-maximization model for what it is: commodifying every aspect of life (everything has a price; a stranger's hand always in a stranger's pocket), leading to, if not accelerating, some of our most-pressing disintegrative crises (think the global economic crisis of 2007, or the austerity crisis of modern Europe). It is here at this point that disruptive change permits us the freedom of raw creativity and innovation to design and construct new economic syntheses with a greater utility other than maximizing value.

CHANGING THE RULES

As disintegration proceeds, disruption is creating our most pivotal opportunity on at least one key ground; imagination. As disintegration extensively envelops old power's economic and political infrastructures, we can expect an increasing disillusionment questioning the relevancy of modern structural models. Crises will grow in size and scope, and the ineffectiveness of obsolete thinking will fail to assuage disintegration. This inevitably opens the door for a fresh set of perspectives—to change the rules; that is, systems, values, and structures—without worry of political expediency. The notion that "there is no alternative"[33], that "the fact that no one has come up with an alternative to the Wall Street crash of 2008...,"[34] and that the world can only work one way, that what is now will always be, is done. Disruptive change, which is a result in itself of innovation and creativity, now gifts us with a chance to apply this imagination to other sectors of society whose demands have diverged from the past three hundred years. To bring the "open source" initiative for example from technology to commerce; emphasizing new systems that act more like networks—open, transparent and interconnected (i.e., new power)—as opposed to pyramids—closed, ambiguous and leader driven (i.e., old power). A good example of this potential is embodied within the Internet that has eliminated some of the old monopolies of capital of the previous wave—many Internet startups can be initiated with investments of only a few hundred dollars; the next Fortune 500 company sitting at a laptop in a coffee shop. If there were to be a systematic extension of this kind of liberality within future economies, new models foreshadow a greater capacity for financial freedom if our economic and legal environment makes the harnessing of the potential of entrepreneurialism easier.

Nevertheless the ultimate objective of disruptive change and the influence of new power upon economics should be its ability to transport global citizen's primary efforts and concerns from survival—avoiding hunger, poverty, homelessness, and so on—to exploration, creativity, and prosperity generally; the things that make life greater. With almost half of the world in poverty[35] (including developed countries) and an estimated 795 million undernourished[36], the future success of the twenty-first century requires more than a shallow attempt at sustainability; this is old-power thinking for there is nothing to sustain.

However this transition occurs, disruption is going to change the rules of the modern world globally. What does this mean? For one, it means that old power's values in the next economic synthesis won't do; this implies an end to the value-maximization ecosystem—that is; the growth and expansion of money as the sole purpose of commerce (which at its essence is about trading goods not currency)—and its sociocultural dominance over the ethics of everyday life. While at present we work for money, go to school for money, sometimes (or maybe most times) choose lovers and marry for money, campaign for it for public offices, go into debt for money, lose friends over it, and so on, disruptive change increasingly makes us weary of the pecuniary burden of our physical existence. It's as if, under the old power ethic, there is a series of taxes and fees associated with simply being alive. However, under the next economic synthesis this narrative is fallacy. And while it may have been tolerable for past generations, the emerging psychosphere is leaning toward new generation's ill content to trade time (i.e., their lives) for money. For the future of global citizens, there must be something more; we want to thrive not just survive.

Thus, if the conversion of new powers ethics succeed, terms like *standard of living* broadly used as a way of describing the central meaning of life—ones value inherently determined by their net worth—will ultimately cease in the next wave as unfit and inflammatory.

As the fruits of disruption gradually mature we could expect to see a greater decentralization of institutions (an end to bureaucracy; though not totally), the proliferation of micro-entrepreneurship (including small family corporations) in contrast to traditional employment, regional (even national) economies whose energy dependencies lie upon eco-friendly resources (as opposed to the antiquated oil energy systems), and more. And though these are intuitive estimations, we are enthusiastic because the present evolutionary shift in values and the physical requirements of the next wave point toward a synthesis that is just as pioneering and experimental for solving problems as it is for commodifying them; commerce that produces solutions not just products; and an ethic that pursues innovation for its own sake, regardless of profitability.

Deconstructing the State

—⚒—

WHAT DISRUPTIVE CHANGE AND DISINTEGRATION are increasingly doing is exposing the vulnerabilities of old-power political models: of representative and parliamentarian governance, of big spending, welfare-state problem solving, of corporatocracy in the international age, and so forth. Ultimately, it exposes a perhaps painful but timely truth that "the state is hopelessly out of date."[37] Though this obsolescence differs from country to country what doesn't differ are the environmental shifts universally encompassing models of government that have been slow to adapt. With the diversification of societies has followed the loss of consensus (including deep partisanship[38]; e.g., the 2016 US election, and the lack of EU solidarity), and subsequently, the political majorities imperative to traditional democracies.[39] Add this to the fact that though the next wave will embrace the decentralization of institutions generally, the state violates the law of motion (growing in size and responsibility), making its bureaucracy inefficient in the process and frustrating progress. As disintegrative crises compile one upon the other, we've consequently witnessed government grow progressively reactionary and paranoid, ultimately becoming a threat to both our preconceived notions of democracy and to itself; increasingly distrustful of its own subjects—as mass surveillance, Snowden versus the National Security Agency, police brutality and questions of net neutrality show. And as public cynicism toward the state and its representatives are reflections of these facts,[40] the legitimacy of government is incrementally compromised on account of its inability to prove culpable—that is, to prove that government is not, inherently, insane (doing the same thing over and over again and expecting a different result).

This intermixed streak of gridlock and the draconian is not the result of a few bad apples in the way, but rather, a consequence of changing circumstances in the universe and government's continual attempts to transfer decrepit methodologies purposed for one era into another. This is to say that government is not only out of date, but it's also stuck. "The state is stuck in the industrial age, it's stuck in the age of huge vertical integration in which it has to own every-thing it provides, own every service."[41] It's stuck in Depression-era crisis relief; the state has been overspending for decades—Keynes's theory of stimulus spending was used as a response to disaster (i.e., the Great Depression), yet governments spend in the same manner as a condition of life, regardless of circumstances. And the state is stuck in welfare political schemes (an industrial era infrastructure), attempting to legislate for a splintered single-issue electorate de-manding privileges while attempting to protect its own interests. In short, government is still grasping the imminent actuality that twen-tieth-century politics is over, along with the intellectual impulses and its institutions that predate it—ideas that are pre-Freud, Marx, or Darwin.[42] In plainer terms, the state cannot attempt to proactively govern the body politick of the twenty-first century with constitutions written and intended to meet the needs and circumstances of hun-dreds of years ago; the witless conservatism that maintains this status quo only leads to greater folly as we dig deeper into the new millen-nium. Thus, as the late Herbert Stein wrote, "If something cannot go on forever it will stop."[43] And the state will stop! Thus, at this point, there are at least two things that cannot, or will not, go on forever: the world cannot keep having mounting inequality, and government cannot keep going as it is without some form of methodical change. We are subsequently forced into a decisive dilemma: either the state progresses with the times or we regress with the state.

As of now, history repeats itself while we emerge into the next historical cycle and the state, for all intents and purposes, is in competition. With the dynamics of power continually shifting, we find that not only is power changing characteristically—that is, in how we define it, how it's used, and who has it in societies—it's also changing geographically. While the twenty-first century experiences an unprecedented wealth shift from the rich world to emerging markets (the next economic synthesis), there is simultaneously a subtle but persistent psychological and ideological struggle vying to shape the next millennia, and the West no longer enjoys a monopoly. Simply put, the future of power is multipolar; the result of the increasing diversification of political authority. John Micklethwait and Adrian Wooldridge who cowrote *The Fourth Revolution: The Global Race to Reinvent the State* present a deliciously controversial premise: that we are in the midst of a new revolution to reinvent government, and the West is being left behind.[44] This is particularly interesting because it was as equally assumed that there existed no alternative for liberal democracies as it was for global capitalism. But if there's one thing we know, nothing lasts forever. While disruptive change has left some governments in states of delirium, there are others, ahead of the curve, which recognize the gravitational pull demanding fundamental transformations in governance. As the dynamics of power rearrange themselves in both hemispheres, this is especially true of China where there are people thinking very hard about government—deconstructing it, reconstructing it, and over again—and who have a very real sense of competition, unlike their counterparts. Disruption has inspired or motivated the Chinese to think and act ahead of the curve—that is, in thinking differently about government we will depart, much like China, from the Eurocentric, Western-style ideas of traditional statehood for something as yet undefined. Micklethwait and Wooldridge pick up on this trend remarking in the *Wall Street Journal*:

> Better government has long been one of the West's great advantages. Now the Chinese want that title back.

Western policy makers should look at this effort the same way that Western businessmen looked at Chinese factories in the 1990s: with a mixture of awe and fear. Just as China deliberately set out to remaster the art of capitalism, it is now trying to remaster the art of government. The only difference is a chilling one: Many Chinese think there is far less to be gained from studying Western government than they did from studying Western capitalism. They visit Silicon Valley and Wall Street, not Washington, D.C.[45]

And this pandering for new thinking extends beyond the shores of Asia. There is an international itch for deconstructing and reimagining the state in both emerging markets and in one's that our critical analysis cannot yet anticipate.

What we're seeing now is a competition between two different economic models which those emerging markets could choose. Do they choose the model of Western democracy or Western Liberalism, or do they choose the alternative competing democracy of top-down, authoritarian, Mandarin-led modernization which is there in China. And as I wonder around the world I'm very struck by the number of people in emerging countries which say, "Actually, the model that we want to base ourselves on is China, not America."[46]

While this is by no means near the end of disruption, nor is it to say that the proto-Communist hybrid of Chinese government is the ideal of future statecraft—to the contrary, the repressive policies of the Chinese state may hinder its potential in an era demanding greater liberality—merging powers have begun to rethink government at its core. Far more than an archetypal rivalry between the West and the East; this serves as a foreshadowing of events. The struggle for the state, as it becomes increasingly pronounced, will ultimately become the struggle

for the soul of the twenty-first century and beyond, just as the tumultuous periods that gave us our present institutions. Subsequently, "the
contest of the twenty-first century is not really to see who comes out on
the top economically or politically, but it is to see who comes out on
top ideologically."[47]

Not only will we witness the deconstruction of the state, but we
will also witness its regeneration, which will refashion the frameworks
of governments as perhaps we've not yet seen. Disruptive change is
rendering the old models of government—particularly traditional democracy—unfit for the next political ecosystem as "democracies, particularly America, but mostly Europe, have become lazy, self-indulgent
and paralyzed," such that an international audience observes the old-
power models and remark how "Europe [for example] is democrati-
cally dysfunctional [and] nobody really likes it,"[48] or how Congress
can't pass budgets. It is, in essence, the breakdown of representative
democracy as a result of changes in the economic, technological and
social demands of societies. While the development of new states persist in thoughtful incubation, the future of government seems split
between whether to move power up (technocracy), move power down
(direct democracy), or somehow execute both. This is particularly interesting as philosophers (principally of the West) have historically
disputed the legitimacy of democracy in its most potent forms; that
it's too short term (individual self-interest and immediate gratification
above the long-term interest of future generations) and dependent on
the crowd—gravitating more toward a mob mentality and away from
reason. As Wooldridge argues, this is a challenging dilemma because
the House of Representatives and Congress embody some of the "defects" of democratic government (focused on the short term, angry,
and volatile), while the European Union embodies the defects of technocracy—that is, all decisions being made by technocrats regardless
of popular votes.[49] Thus, the struggle of our time is in finding the balance—equilibrium in the dynamics of power. It is here that disruptive
change presents new power its opportunity to enter the picture.

THE NEXT POLITICAL FRONTIER

The test for new power, therefore, isn't just about its will to power—that is, whether it can do more than change short-term political dynamics—but also how it reacts once the dynamics of power do change—that is, what happens to new power when it becomes powerful, if at all. A challenge for democratic thinking of itself in that postdisruption, new power or variants thereof must prove its political competency in its ability to generate results; to depart from the shortcomings of democracy's surplus in rhetoric and slogans but its deficit in pragmatic action, the ability to fulfill on promises made before office. For example, we take an analogy from Heimans; i.e., the Obama campaign vs. the Obama presidency. Upon running for the presidency, Obama used the power of crowds (i.e., new-power values) with slogans—"Change We Can Believe In," "Yes We Can," "Hope," and "Forward"—to insinuate sentiments of optimism, unity, and a wave of change from the bottom up among a disillusioned and apathetic electorate, using youth as his base of support and his legitimacy to candidacy. "But when he got into office, he governed like more or less the other presidents did."[50] The "populist"-like change succumbed to business as usual. Nevertheless, our preceding discourse on changes in the psychosphere and its effects upon the economic synthesis point toward a new political frontier that is multipolar both horizontally (greater hegemony across states; countries like Brazil, India, Russia, China, and South Africa) and vertically (greater hegemony among people in society).

As demassification continues, the role of governments will have to adjust themselves to an increasing demand by global citizens for greater participation and influence in political and commercial affairs. Old-power influences established the auspices of representation and parliamentarianism as the most efficient means to govern people and enact policies that would lead, in a mass society, to the general good. But not only is autonomy a valuable ethic financially or socially, many citizens of the United States, for example, feel they can do a better job of enforcing their political interests than their political representatives[51]; a consequence of low esteem for the state. So while the tenets of representative or parliamentarian democracy monopolized government models, twenty-first-century innovations will likely replace these institutions and their forms entirely (though there's no way to estimate how long this will take). The challenge, therefore, will be for the state to balance the dynamics of power between direct democracy and technocratic institutions, which will be a difficult adjustment.

On one end, while the idea of majoritarian rule sufficed for industrial mass societies, in the direct democracy of the next wave, we'll swap minority rule in its place—the splintering of consensus having made mobilizing majorities impractical. Under these conditions, larger political coalitions are replaced by smaller, often temporary partnerships by thousands of minorities who seldom have a 51 percent consensus on major issues.[52] And while majority rule might have meant a "fair break" for states more conscious of difference in class or social standing, the opposite is true as numbers do not guarantee political victory; the marriage equality battle is a great example of this (a classic minority victory). Thus, there is emerging a new directly democratic ethic that will in due time reduce the significance of representative politicians—one cannot pose to speak for a majority that doesn't exist, much less actually represent their disparate interests—for the initiative of the individual and the special-interest minority. As these changes gradually take place this will likely lead to prolonged struggles to recondition domestic institutions like Congress, Houses of Commons and Lords, the Bundestag, French National Assembly, Diet, and their international equivalents in the UN and EU, all the way down to local councils and municipalities. The future of statecraft in the new millennium therefore depends largely on how it manages and either concedes or resists the thrust of greater hegemony from below. This includes the gradual demand for a more intimate style of leadership in the modern age; tomorrow's leaders must be more accessible and transparent as compared to the traditional ambiguousness of republican institutions—the future of governance and harmony between states and their citizens depend significantly on this evolutionary adjustment. How peaceful this transition will be is unfore-seeable at present; depending, among other things, upon the flexibility or obstinacy of modern elites, the occurrence of economic catastrophe, or the potential for conflict of war.

On the other hand, though demassification is accelerating the signifi-cance of a new form of democratic participation, not all decisions can be deliberated upon locally or at a democratic level. The existence of some form of private power is not optional but necessary, especially in the area of international affairs—something new power must capitulate. Thus, the state must find its technocratic niche expeditiously as the increasing inte-gration of national and international affairs becomes a defining feature of the next wave. One problem requires solutions in areas seemingly unre-lated to the original dilemma; isolation as an aspect of any national policy has now lost its relevance. This has become true for every facet of the social organism. No longer can government elaborate on transportation without also elaborating on energy and environmental health, just as multination-als can no longer concern themselves primarily with exploiting oil without also considering the political and social consequences of their actions upon international stability or the interest of constituents at home.

So what does this mean—uncertainty, political pessimism, crises? Disintegration has already presented us with these. Instead, we are op-timistically presented with an opportunity of a lifetime—chance dis-coveries influencing at least a century. The thirst for new models and thinking is a quest to remake government for the twenty-first century, and the state is thereby ready for deconstruction. This means, among other things, our inventing of new forms and the end of "democracy for export" as the single geopolitical standard of modernization and civil-ity, thus permitting greater diversity of state models internationally. As disruptive change upends the international status quo, we will inevitably be reminded, as new forms emerge, that the world works in more ways than one. New power's emphasis on transparency, decentralization, do-it-yourself, and the power of crowds thus gives us the chance to reimag-ine and re-create conceptions of statehood and nationhood universally.

While the necessity of the technocratic imperative, or its variants, will act as the opposing charge able to bring balance to the emerging order.

Thus, in the process of outgrowing the obsolete traditions and contradictions of old-power rule, we'll be hard pressed to ask in-depth philosophical questions about the way we're governed. New power will have to address the modern state's paranormal condition, its penchant for mass surveillance, police violence and totalitarian behavior. We have long accepted surveillance as a normal by-product of "civilized" life and slowly and seductively have adopted pathological forms as the norm, without realizing that aberrant methods of "record-keeping"— social security numbers, academic and criminal records, credit histories, browsing and call histories, consumer reports, and so on—are manifestations not only of the state's proclivity to monitor its citizens, but its conscious and unconscious distrust of them as well. Global citizens' collective rise or fall therefore will be in its ability, or inability, to find a balance between security and privacy in a transparent world; to deal with the root of our dilemmas—particularly, the underlying psychosis of fear characterizing modern statehood—not the symptoms, both at a state level and one of social consciousness. A disturbed government only reproduces a disturbed society, which subsequently leads to the development of a backward civilization in its various forms, and from this the new millennium must depart. Global citizens must work with their governments, not for them. And there is much reason to argue the potential for the development of smaller states in the future, as Micklethwait and Wooldridge assert.

> The overloaded modern state is a threat to democracy: The more responsibilities Leviathan assumes, the worse it performs them, and the angrier citizens get. Such a state is also a threat to liberty: When the state takes half of everything that you produce and regulates the smallest details of daily life, it has become a master rather than a servant. Better to do fewer things—and to do them better.[53]

This ultimately represents a hypothetical shot at our archaic governance institutions, whose practical legitimacy should be heavily disputed. That is, in an era where without threat of war, civil strife, or revolution, governments literally "shut down" in bureaucratic and partisan stalemates—an era where politicians vacillate in indecision concerning issues that matter.

Of all the idiosyncrasies accompanying the processes of disruption, the deconstructing and reordering of governments will perhaps be the most impactful yet most painful of all changes that will take place. Politics is messy—period. And it's messy because of the reality that there exist at least three kinds of people: those who accept change, those who don't, and those who go with whatever's convenient at the time. Nevertheless, we have entered a critical period where there are select groups of people critically rethinking and experimenting about the role of government in society around the world—this includes what it has been, what it has not been, and what it could, or rather should, be. Regardless of which "camp" one belongs to, there is a revolutionary change increasingly applying pressure to old power's political structures and the simultaneous development of newfangled innovations, or crises, in technology, the environment, energy, international political economy, and finance, which only accelerates the pressure for deconstruction and the necessity of regeneration.

Freedom over Order

—◊—

WHEN WRITING WHERE NEW AND Old Power Combine, Anthony Painter opens with a relevant statement: "We are in an era of a profound shift in the nature of social and political power. The power structures of the twentieth century, reliant on hierarchical, technocratic methods, are weakening."[54] This is to say, old power and its muses are dwindling, even disintegrating, but not dead. In the midst of a crisis of time, where a matured era collides with one in the process of birth, we are faced with many difficult questions and equally arduous answers. Nevertheless, looking inwardly toward an uncertain future, we can be sure of at least two things: the present is past, and these are undoubtedly extraordinary times. The future, in a word, requires transcendence. We cannot, in the false comforts of nostalgia, rely upon customs, traditions, and think-ing far gone; the winds of change have collectively cornered our planet. We are therefore faced with two choices: to gradually evolve into some-thing greater or decline. It is of less importance whether humankind will transform, because this we can be sure of; of more concern is what we transform into. Disruptive change is not merely an artificial slogan of some kind to give credibility to phenomena that do not exist; disrup-tion is real. We are witnesses of disruptive innovations in every facet of personal and social life: the YouTubes, the Kickstarters, the Ubers, the Airbnbs, the Apples, the Facebooks, the Twitters, and so on. However, we are also witnesses of the crises: the economic and financial calamities, the deficiencies of modern governance, the conflicts of international relations, the violence, the surveillance, the pessimism, and the apathy. If this were only a case of transformative breakthroughs in technology and business, or just bad apples, we'd have less to talk about. We'd be conspiring over the best ways to take advantage of the markets, to ride the waves of change for our profit, the next big bubble, and the next big thing. Or we'd speak of campaigning for reform. However, this is far more than a good business idea, some amusing technology that offsets our loneliness and boredom, or a moral crusade; this is the accumulative integration of events shaping the next historical cycle—the type of change that could obliterate the very concept of markets and bubbles just as fast as they came.

Even though disruption will inevitably lead to the eventual decline of old power, our principal dilemma lies in what takes its place. As the possibilities of new power remain imminent, its future is still uncertain. Having proven itself effective by means of rhetoric we have still to witness, despite the growing extensiveness of disruptive change, new power's ability to significantly alter the fundamental fabric of old-power civilization. In a number of cases, we've instead observed the integration of disruptive innovations into the formulaic systems of the last wave—a "selling out" literally or figuratively. Therefore, the challenge of the future for new power is twofold in that as a power phenomenon, it must prove capable of producing intended effects (without participation and a clear direction, new-power models are inept); and when it manages to do so, it mustn't repeat the tyrannies of the past or create greater ones for the future. That means balancing the desire for democratization and the feasibility of closed-door, technocratic problem solving. "There's a fine line between democratizing participation and a mob mentality"[55]; therefore, new power must transcend the fickle character of twentieth-century mass thinking. This means that, while we desire to be liberated from the hoops of old-power society—its rules, standards, and endless procedures—new-power civilization must determine, definitely, its basis for existence. Each civilization is collectively gifted, or cursed, with the freedom of choice—that is to say, the opportunity to determine their underlying rationale, whether it exists in the name of equality, balance, liberty or order. The previous wave that is old power begot a world that valued order over anything else. For all its lip service to liberty, opportunity, democracy, and innovation, we are the progeny of doctrines of conformity; "old power is enabled by what people or organizations own, know, or control that nobody else does."[56] It is a backward form in which secret advantages, justified around a doctrine of scarcity, are the keys to wealth and power within infrastructures engineered to maintain, if not enhance, inequalities. But as the young adult who escapes the neatly packaged ecosystem of childhood, we find that it's a different world than where we come from and yearn for more than the prism that this monotony can provide. Unlike the last-wave civilizations, the new wave espouses a different value: freedom, freedom from all limitation—that is, freedom over order. For all its magnificent innovations, breakthroughs, discoveries, and praises, the drudgeries of life for the greater part of humanity under old power make them of less comparison. Even though our TV screens may tell a different, even dramatized story, we in the new wave have purposes, desires, and yearnings other than working to pay bills and voting for political elites every two or four years. Moreover, we reemphasize that we are here to change the world—not just follow rules, earn money, and die. And at long last, with disruptive change as the catalyst and new power as the vehicle, we are presented the opportune moment to release ourselves of the bonds of old-power civilization—its thinking, principles, attitudes, habits, and nuances—in order that we may be creators, in the purest sense, of the next wave that is to be the twenty-first century and beyond in the spirit of freedom.

OLD POWER AS BACKWARD CIVILIZATION

As with any conflicting set of values, the new wave stands hindered by the obstacles of the last. We have an undying desire to be free. However, old power has bound us—intentionally by its character and inadvertently by its design—with its obstacles and its need for conformity, obedience,

economic growth, and value—that is, for control. In an era struggling
for freedom, the old world view cannot cohabitate lest it diminishes our
chances of self-determination by way of its backwardness. As our under-
standings of the world differ, its maxims appear perverse, contrary to
the natural flow of things. This is because a world view is no more than
a reflection of the dominant opinions of power at a certain time—something disruptive change is altering each passing day. Inevitably, disruption and disintegration draw us to a new wave that differs equally in ends
as it does in means with the last. This comes at a time when the artificial
veil of liberty—used by old power to mask its obsession for control—is
being rent to pieces. Thus, we are now compelled to correct those historical wrongs that have rendered old-power civilizations as backward.

The next wave is one that will require the absence of all limitations—
legal, political, economic, social, and so forth—as a condition of freedom (not to be confused with liberty); conditions presently hindered by
a disintegrating infrastructure built for other means. If new power is to
be a factor in the twenty-first century and beyond, it must change the
governing dynamics of our universe at its core. This implies the transformation of many things, among them the restructuring of the state
form, which has done more to obstruct its subjects than relieve them.
We yearn to escape the paternalistic statism that is modern governance,
the one that argues "it's not enough to just step away and leave people
alone, as a libertarian...would and simply trust emergent community
alone."[57] The one that condescendingly asserts that "sometimes the state
should get out of the way by removing legal, administrative, or procedur-
al hurdles"[58] in the spirit of entitlement. Disruption has fed us through
with the paradoxical conundrum that is modern governance—the state
model that believes in placing hurdles before its citizens to begin with.
Exposing the vulnerabilities of majoritarian democracy (drawn more
toward conformity and a mob mentality) change calls for the departure
of mass politics, which obstructs the capabilities of new power by virtue
of its inadequacy—the micro replacing the macro. The crisis of representative government as a twentieth-century life-form isn't merely a

reflection of a crisis in the moment but also a testament of its incapacity to rule justly—rule being a moral ethic disruption is discarding.

With new power pending, the next political frontier foreshadows a synthesis in which the represented represent themselves, as only they can do best—meaning, away with the dualism of our political rituals. Therefore, the new state is conveyed best through autonomy and self-determination. Thus, far apart from any dogmatic egalitarianism, the politics of new power in the next wave will succeed best through an absence of artificial constraint—that is, freedom from control (elite, mob, or otherwise). These are the same principles that disruption, in conjunction with our cry for freedom, calls us to apply to our commercial affairs, to leave the psychopathological obstacles presented by value maximization as the underlying element of exchange activity. The next wave will be responsible for restoring balance to models of commerce in disequilibrium that overemphasize monetary value as the primary end of trade and exchange. The value-maximization theories and models, in the process of commodifying all social life, limited civilizations' capacities for innovation, creativity, and out-of-the-box thought, thus incarcerating human potential under a dictatorship of currency. Money became the standard by which inspiration, vision, and inventiveness are measured, perverting the purity of artistry in a free world by limiting genius to its profitability with value maximization as a form of control. Therefore, our urge for freedom compels us to be emancipated from the underlying motif of maximizing value as the ultimate thrust of progress in society—the sacrificing of creative genius to the whims of shrewd business sense. As new power matures and finds balance in its preference for participation, the future will witness the dethronement of the international system of currency and its demand for infinite growth as the gatekeepers of mobility, creativity, and autonomy. That is to say, we will create, absent of monetary incentives, because creation, provided it is constructive, is good in itself. Disruption thus leads us to a new ethic in the spirit of freedom: creativity and innovation for its own sake.

As disruptive change creates space for new power to establish a millennium of liberation, both for humankind as social beings and as individuals, we are called to more. Therefore, above all that disruptive change will do in the absence of all limitations—political, economic, or legal—freedom fills us with a momentous impetus for the removal of all limitations on life. The future is one where generations will not merely be able to fantasize about questions such as "What do I desire?" or "What if money were no object?"—as old-power civilization only permitted us to do—but will, in the full embrace of freedom, enable us to pursue and acquire the fullness of our desires. The end of disruption being, in essence, the creation of a *new genesis* for a world that will settle for no less than its full self-determination—even nature itself. This means liberation from the repressions of an old-power world and its mechanistic Newtonian philosophy undergirding modern civilization's nihilism. Disruption has thus rendered the era of the ego—man as omniscient, omnipotent ruler of matter—as inoperative by virtue of its unsophisticated approach to the material world. Replacing societal illusions—its linear conception of time (beginning to end), its longitudes and latitudes, its mistaking the accumulation of money for wealth, its nine-to-fives, its office politics, its rush hours, its rules, its codes of conduct, its false deference, its need for conformity, its taboos, its obstacles, its pressures, its propensity to control nature than to leave it be—with a balanced order, in all its freedom. The only control in the next wave is over oneself. Thus, disruptive change has rendered the disintegration of old power as an emancipating moment for nature as equally as it is for its inhabitants. All winds of change point toward freedom. The success, therefore, of new power in the new millennium will be a representation of our ability, as global citizens, as unique people, to reach our full potential in a free world—capacities hardly maximized by the control-centered civilizations of the last wave. Therefore, our impetus for freedom is no more than a product of our desire to stop wasting our time, to relieve in a world of distraction and duty (compelled by a fear of poverty) both ourselves and the future generations of the burden that has been old power.

Disintegration merely perpetuates the natural process to which all life-forms are subject—transience, impermanent existence. Although these appear as strong positions to take, these are no ordinary times. For the change makers of our time, disruption presents us a great exhalation from the tensions enforced by the doctrines and principles of an age now past. We are enthralled with a sense of destiny to be creators in the purest sense of the word as our predecessors—who bequeathed the institutions we take for granted—did in their time. *"Caught between two civilizations, it was their destiny to create,"* *and now it is ours at every level, "of social life, in our families, in our schools, our business and churches, in our energy systems and communications, we face the need to create new Third Wave forms."*[59] There has never been a better time to be alive.

Thus, in the spirit of autonomy and in the absence of limitations inspired by disruption, we give ourselves to new maxims. As articulated by the late Alan Watts, "In some way or other, the human race has to learn to leave the world alone,"[60] including ourselves. Therefore, as apprentices of disruptive change, we have no ten-point principles but just one requirement: freedom.

To an opportune present and a limitless future;
laissez-faire as a philosophy of life.

References

—⚏—

1. B. F. Skinner, *Walden Two*, (New York: Macmillan, 1976).
2. Abdul Kalam, "182. A. P. J. ABDUL KALAM: Life's Pursuit," *ZEN PENCILS*, August 17, 2015, accessed October 14, 2015, http://zenpencils.com/comic/kalam/.
3. Charles Darwin, "Charles Darwin Quotes," *Thinkexist.com*, accessed October 14, 2015, http://thinkexist.com/quotation/it_is_not_the_strongest_of_the_species_that/7533.html.
4. Deepak Chopra, "Deepak Chopra Quotes," *Deepak Chopra Quotes* (author of *The Seven Spiritual Laws of Success*), accessed October 14, 2015, http://www.goodreads.com/quotes/783959-every-great-change-is-preceded-by-chaos.
5. Shiv Malik, "Adults in Developing Nations More Optimistic than Those in Rich Countries," *The Guardian*, April 14, 2014, accessed June 14, 2016, http://www.theguardian.com/politics/2014/apr/14/developing-nations-more-optimistic-richer-countries-survey.
6. Ibid.
7. Jeremy Heimans, "What New Power Looks Like," *TED*, June 1, 2014, accessed October 14, 2015, https://www.ted.com/talks/jeremy_heimans_what_new_power_looks_like?language=en.
8. Ibid.
9. Ibid.
10. D'Vera Cohn, and Andrea Caumont, "10 Demographic Trends That Are Shaping the U.S. and the World," Pew Research Center RSS, March 31, 2016, accessed June 10, 2016, http://www.pewresearch.

org/fact-tank/2016/03/31/10-demographic-trends-that-are-shaping-the-u-s-and-the-world/.

11. Richard Fry, "A Rising Share of Young Adults Live in Their Parents' Home," Pew Research Centers Social Demographic Trends Project RSS, August 1, 2013, accessed June 11, 2016, http://www.pewsocialtrends.org/2013/08/01/a-rising-share-of-young-adults-live-in-their-parents-home/.

12. "Data Story: Millennials Infographic." Goldman Sachs. 2013. Accessed June 11, 2016. http://www.goldmansachs.com/our-thinking/pages/millennials/.

13. Ibid.

14. Cohn and Caumont, "10 Demographic Trends That Are Shaping the U.S. and the World."

15. Ibid.

16. Benjamin Wormald, "U.S. Public Becoming Less Religious," Pew Research Centers Religion Public Life Project RSS, November 3, 2015, accessed June 17, 2016, http://www.pewforum.org/2015/11/03/u-s-public-becoming-less-religious/.

17. Rebecca Harris, "The Loneliness Epidemic: We're More Connected than Ever—but Are We Feeling More Alone?" *The Independent*, March 30, 2015, accessed June 17, 2016, http://www.independent.co.uk/life-style/health-and-families/features/the-loneliness-epidemic-more-connected-than-ever-but-feeling-more-alone-10143206.html.

18. Alvin Toffler, "The New Psycho-Sphere," in *The Third Wave* (New York: Morrow, 1980), 369.

19. Heimans, "What New Power Looks Like."

20. Henry Timms, "What New Power Is…and Three Things It Is Not," Weforum.org, June 10, 2016, accessed November 20, 2014, https://www.weforum.org/agenda/2014/11/what-new-power-is-and-three-things-it-is-not/.

21. Heimans, "What New Power Looks Like."

22. Albert Einstein, "Albert Einstein Quotes," *Goodreads*, accessed October 15, 2015, http://www.goodreads.com/quotes/320600-we-cannot-solve-our-problems-with-the-same-level.

23. Cade Metz, "Thought Bitcoin Was Dead? 2016 Is the Year It Goes Big," Wired.com, January 5, 2016, accessed June 26, 2016, http://www.wired.com/2016/01/thought-bitcoin-was-dead-2016-is-the-year-it-goes-big/.

24. Robert McMillan, "The Inside Story of Mt. Gox, Bitcoin's $460 Million Disaster," Wired.com, March 3, 2014, accessed June 26, 2016, http://www.wired.com/2014/03/bitcoin-exchange/.

25. Dani Rodrik, "Emerging Markets: The End of Growth?" Chicago Council on Global Affairs, April 5, 2016, accessed June 28, 2016, https://www.thechicagocouncil.org/event/emerging-markets-end-growth.

26. "GDP Annual Growth Rate | Forecast | 2016–2020," GDP Annual Growth Rate | Forecast | 2016–2020, March 1, 2016, accessed June 28, 2016, http://www.tradingeconomics.com/forecast/gdp-annual-growth-rate.

27. Rob Asghar, "Study: Millennials Are the True Entrepreneur Generation," *Forbes*, November 11, 2014, accessed June 29, 2016, http://www.forbes.com/sites/robasghar/2014/11/11/study-millennials-are-the-true-entrepreneur-generation/#291c3b985e92.

28. Bentley University, "Millennials at Work," Millennial Minds: The PreparedU Project Survey, November 11, 2014, accessed June 29, 2016, http://www.bentley.edu/newsroom/latest-headlines/mind-of-millennial.

29. Toffler, "Decoding the New Rules," 260.

30. Ibid, 260–1.

31. Richard Florida, "The 25 Most Economically Powerful Cities in the World," CityLab, September 15, 2011, accessed June 29, 2016, http://www.citylab.com/work/2011/09/25-most-economically-powerful-cities-world/109/#slide4.

32. Toffler, "Decoding the New Rules," 260.

33. Wikipedia, s.v. "There Is No Alternative," last modified June 9, 2016, accessed June 30, 2016, https://en.wikipedia.org/wiki/There_is_no_alternative.

34. Laura Flanders, "At Thatcher's Funeral, Bury TINA, Too," *The Nation*, April 12, 2013, accessed June 30, 2016, https://www.thenation.com/article/thatchers-funeral-bury-tina-too/.

35. Anup Shah, "Poverty Facts and Stats," Global Issues, January 7, 2013, accessed July 1, 2016, http://www.globalissues.org/article/26/poverty-facts-and-stats.

36. "Hunger Statistics | WFP | United Nations World Food Programme—Fighting Hunger Worldwide," Hunger Statistics | WFP | United Nations World Food Programme—Fighting Hunger Worldwide, accessed July 1, 2016, https://www.wfp.org/hunger/stats.

37. John Micklethwait and Adrian Wooldridge, "The Fourth Revolution: The Global Race to Reinvent the State," YouTube, May 22, 2014, accessed October 15, 2015, https://www.youtube.com/watch?v=E2sDnfoC3Hk.

38. Carroll Doherty and Jocelyn Kiley, "Key Facts about Partisanship and Political Animosity in America," Pew Research Center RSS, June 22, 2016, accessed July 2, 2016, http://www.pewresearch.org/fact-tank/2016/06/22/key-facts-partisanship/.

39. Alvin Toffler, "The Political Mausoleum," in *The Third Wave* (New York, NY: Morrow, 1980), 410.

40. Hannah Fingerhut, "Beyond Distrust: How Americans View Their Government," Pew Research Center for the People and the Press RSS, November 23, 2015, accessed July 2, 2016, http://www.people-press.org/2015/11/23/beyond-distrust-how-americans-view-their-government/.

41. Micklethwait and Wooldridge, "The Fourth Revolution: The Global Race to Reinvent the State," YouTube.

42. Toffler, "The Political Mausoleum," 414.

43. Herbert Stein, *What I Think: Essays on Economics, Politics, and Life* (Washington, DC: AEI Press, 1998).

44. John Micklethwait and Adrian Wooldridge, *The Fourth Revolution: The Global Race to Reinvent the State* (New York: Penguin Books, 2014).

45. John Micklethwait and Adrian Wooldridge, "Can China Best the West at Statecraft?" *Wall Street Journal*, May 16, 2014, accessed October 15, 2015, http://www.wsj.com/articles/SB100014240527023045477045 79562230042916694.

46. Micklethwait and Wooldridge, "The Fourth Revolution: The Global Race to Reinvent the State," YouTube.

47. Ibid.

48. Ibid.

49. Ibid.

50. Heimans, "What New Power Looks like."

51. Fingerhut, "Beyond Distrust: How Americans View Their Government."

52. Alvin Toffler, "Twenty-First Century Democracy," in *The Third Wave* (New York, NY: Morrow, 1980), 420.

53. Micklethwait and Wooldridge, "Can China Best the West at Statecraft?"

54. Anthony Painter, "Blog: Person-to-Person Social Justice—Where New and Old Power Combine," *The RSA*, July 23, 2015, accessed October 15, 2015, https://www.thersa.org/discover/publications-and-articles/rsa-blogs/2015/07/persontopersonpower.

55. Henry Timms, "Understanding New Power," *Harvard Business Review*, December 1, 2014, accessed October 14, 2015, https://hbr.org/2014/12/understanding-new-power.

56. Ibid.

57. Micklethwait and Wooldridge, "The Fourth Revolution: The Global Race to Reinvent the State," YouTube.

58. Ibid.

59. Toffler, "Twenty-First Century Democracy."

60. Alan Watts, "Alan Watts Breaks Down What's Wrong with the World—Part 1 (1970)," YouTube, December 22, 2013, accessed October 15, 2015, https://www.youtube.com/watch?v=_LXiSPpfM54.

About the Author

JULIAN DOCKS IS A TWENTY-TWO-YEAR-OLD serial entrepreneur, designer, and writer. A self-proclaimed futurist, he dropped out of college at nineteen to pursue publications and business outside the classroom. A sucker for philosophy, he believes disruption is not merely an intellectual ideal to be talked about but a principle to be acted upon. *Disruptive Change* is his first book. He currently lives in Chicago.